The
5000 Year Message

From the Designer of Humans

Tom Carr

The 5000 Year Message

Contents

The 5000 Year Message

The 5000 Year Message

Introduction

A couple of years ago, I wasn't expecting anything, and I received a very interesting transmission. This is the book The 5000 Year Message. It arrived in a two hour period one evening in September. I took the dictation after I came back to earth from off-world and didn't know what to do with it, so I just saved the file. This was the start of a series of transmissions I pushed through.

So, off-world we don't have memos. Memos are something you can say you didn't get. Off-world, information is there, all you do is look for information on a subject and you get everything, more info than you can handle in the next decade if you study full time.

I call this body of information a symbol. I had to pick a name or a description, so symbol works. Symbol in this context means all the information about a subject.

The 5000 Year Message

An easy way to think of a symbol is like a neural network where there are a large number of neurons and connections between the neurons can change in strength and number. This universal structure existed before the physical brain and is the model for the brain.

For example, five billion years ago there was no earth or brains upon it, but this symbol structure was already nearly ten billion years in use. On earth we understand a bit about brains, so it's an easy comparison to say that knowledge in the universe is structured like the human brain.

As a dualist, I simply come back from off-world, sit down at the computer, and write down what I remember. I haven't gotten any new transmissions in a while, so maybe this is it and that's fine. I still haven't provided most of the detail, but I've gotten enough for now, and I have the rest of the information if anyone wants it.

Off-world, I guess I would compare myself to a janitor on earth. Hey, I guess someone must do it and I drew the short straw in the forever drawing. The truth I ignore is I'm just a slow learner on a universal scale.

When I was a kid, my family used to go to Huntington Beach in California on summer days. The sun was out, the sand was warm, the water was nice and the waves were big. Everyone liked and loved each other. Those were the best of days.

Because I didn't want them to end, I would stay in the water for one more wave. When everyone was getting ready to leave, I wanted one more wave.

On one trip, everyone had packed up and was in the car and my dad was driving the old Dodge station wagon out of the parking lot and I had to climb into the back as it was moving. I just wanted one more wave, no matter what.

Have you ever wanted something that much? Have you ever had such passion that it overwhelmed you? What can elicit that passion within you? What do you care about so much that you will take action to get it?

On the other hand, I've been here since the last upgrade was done, like forty thousand years ago. Usually, I'm sitting at the back of the room while someone tells us how important they are. They are the going to get whacked, but not before they step all over everyone around them. In all that time, it never has ended well for that person, but the next guy does the same thing. It appears to be an error in the human design, that ego gets inflated proportionate to power, but I assume there is a reason for this design specification.

When I announce off-world I would like to transmit some symbols down to earth, the entities barely look up, the cadres ignore me: "You know the designer's crew has a plan and they are taking care of this, right?"

Yeah, yeah, I know. John Cusack once lamented something like, "no one likes my puppet show." Well, it was a role he delivered, but I identified with him. We could have been contenders.

I'm not being "given" this information. Because I'm active off-world, I can access it just like anyone else off-world, the Archives are always there, the Symbols are always there. Because I'm a dualist, I can stuff it in my mind and retrieve it a bit better than other people, only losing maybe half of it. The secret I know is that if enough of you understand the truth, we can create a portal and get really good things. Lots and lots of really good things you would truly love.

I'm not the only one working on this, though maybe I'm the only one to put it in your face. So, you may hear about some of the stuff I talk about from one place or another. Don't worry about it, the stuff is in the ether, there are lots of us working on the same project. If someone says the same things I'm saying, they are accessing the same Symbol. Their ego may tell them to claim they figured out the universe. I've been there, too, and so will you. Nod and smile, all good.

I've been waiting decades for transmissions, but no one sent me anything. So, I just started doing it myself when I go off-world and come back. My associates off-world say I wasn't ready, or it wasn't the right time before. Whatever.

I've used the symbols I can access to write three books detailing a projection which is a composite of several probable realities. So, I have access to probable realities off-world. It's easy to get access to whichever probable reality matches your vibration or perspective. So, when someone has a near death experience, they are tethered to their body on earth with a silver cord. My dear hero, Yogananda, was able to sever his silver cord from off-world and die just to show the western world how it works. So, these people are dead for a minute and get access to the probable reality which most closely aligns with their vibration. They see what is best for them to see, most often they see the beauty off-world, a religious experience, or a future which is a probable reality. Probable reality does not mean it is the most probable reality, it means given values for specific variables, this is the most likely future.

In my off-world review of probable realities, I have access to more than one probable reality. The one that I resonated with most was the one where we get a wonderful world, even though seven out of ten I looked at were extinction one way or another.

So, as a liaison, I'm presenting what I see as the transmission of symbols which are the antidote to several probable realities which end in human extinction. It was surprising to me. I did not expect that human extinction was impending. You hear about it off-world, but unless the probable reality is the one you hope for, you blow off the rest. This book is To Stop Extinction. I had no plans for such a book or title until it arrived over the course of a couple months.

It's not likely, simply because a good number of humans have to want to be wealthy and secure instead of suffering, and they don't know they have a choice. It will take at least 1 out of every 200

American adults. I hope I can show you how you make a choice instead of being a victim. This is not a creating wealth pep talk; this is a nice tool which is activation of mass consciousness. I'm not sure I'm good enough at this stuff to do it, but I'm going to try. I figure at least you should know this option exists and it's simple to make happen. I brought this option back from off-world because I'm tired of the way some people run this planet, it's not fair and results in extinction.

The 5000 Year Message is the first document of the projection. I was given the assembled version of a guide to being human delivered over the last 5000 years. This delivery was in four events by the designer of humans. My naming of the designer of humans is a functional personification. You can choose any name which you feel is appropriate for the power or consciousness or part of the universe which designed humans.

These four events were for the purpose of delivering a message. These messages were delivered through the best human available at the time for the specific message. Each of the four events resulted in a major religion. These religions are Hinduism, Buddhism, Taoist, and Christianity.

The 5000 Year Message

In The 5000 Year Message, we assemble these four parts into one, which becomes more than the parts: a guide for being human and understanding your experience of life on earth. The assembled message is only about 25 words.

I don't know why the message hadn't been assembled before, these pieces have been lying around for the longest time. Maybe it has been assembled before. It's just common knowledge off-world. As well, I have no idea why I got the transmission, it's not like I'm in the loop on anything big off-world. Still, I think it's cool I did get it, and I hope I have delivered it properly.

In the second book, A Definition of Human Rights, we define human rights from an off-world perspective: there are 25 human rights. Your task is to choose which of these 25 human rights you want for yourself and your family. Your only assurance of getting these rights is if everyone gets these rights. A method of advantage is only temporary because it only benefits you, and we call this mindset Advantagist.

In this third book, To Stop Extinction, we provide examples of Simple Systems which are based on the definitions of human rights. These systems bring wealth and security to everyone. Properly executed, the need for advantage is superseded by wealth and security for everyone. We provide a plan for implementation which provides a good chance of stopping extinction.

The first part of this book is Simple Systems. So, as we all know, we humans do things ass-backwards. The good news is that it is pretty simple to fix if you want to be wealthy and secure. By you, I mean a group of humans. Yeah, I know, don't hold your breath. Humans would have to participate. Ouch, deal breaker.

The third part is a plan to stop extinction, you know, something like a 12- step. How do we get out of this mess. Potentially. Not likely, not even being considered, barely possible. But that's all I have for you. Sorry in advance. The odds are against us.

In all three books, the fourth part, Foundation, is the same. The Foundation is basic off-world information. This is so that anyone can get one book but can get the same overview of the off-world program. While I know this does not follow traditional book publishing concepts, my presentation is not compromised by those traditions, though I do love books.

These off-world books are not static, completed documents, but instead are versioned documents with progressive editions if changes are made. The versioning of the foundation will be noted by number and date, such as Edition 1 July 2022 and then Edition 2 December 2023, etc.

After the basic information in the Foundation, there is a bit about me, so you don't ask who the Hell wrote this. It's at the very end of the book. If you get that far, you may glance over it and close the cover. Fair enough. This section includes my simple description of duality, a bit about my self-appointed role as liaison, and a description of symbols and how I transmit symbols from off-world to earth.

We humans are hurling undauntedly towards extinction and destruction of earth, generally without concern.

The off-world perspective is that two-thirds of species such as humans destroy their planet and themselves. So pending destruction is not a surprise but a likelihood. And it is the 11th hour for humans.

At the same time, 1/3 of species like humans don't destroy themselves. The off-world community is reaching out to help us understand how.

At this point, we face the final test for a free will species. This test is to overcome your instinct to survive without concern for others and instead participate as a part of a whole, the human beings of earth. By design, the tribal instinct is normally weaker than your instinct to survive. The perspective to which we transition is that for any of us to survive, we must all get the same opportunity. If you only focus on your own survival, eventually as a species you destroy the planet because everyone feels their survival is a valid reason to grab whatever they need or want. That time is happening now.

Humans must make this transition in their minds. If we don't, the odds are we will go extinct. So, this is a test of the species design. Are our minds good enough to see the value of others instead of ignoring others? It is within our power to do this, but will we? The answer so far is no.

The purpose of this projection by the off-world community is to offer the means to improve the lives of humans and fix the planet.

In the movie The Day the Earth Stood Still, the arrival of an alien causes global trauma and chaos. We want to fix things but avoid the global trauma and chaos and general killing-off of humans. Any human can scoff at this offer. Scoffing may not be nice, but it does not cause global trauma and chaos.

It may make a good movie that heaven opens, and an angel shows us the way, or a spaceship arrives in Central Park, but there's going to be some chaos. How can it be done without chaos and getting the kids all traumatized? Get a local to make their offer. I guess that would be me.

The off-world community is offering you wealth, a better quality of life, incredible technology, amazing, large scale environmental solutions, and solutions to social problems.

Right now, I have access to about 50 technologies. I don't have them sitting at home, I have access, I can get them in the right situation. Now, some may show up in the meantime, as I said, I'm not the only circus in town. They are giving this stuff away. So, that is a pretty good deal. I am just the liaison, a facilitator or broker.

It will take some work to save this species and fixing the planet will take a lot of work. To explain what is offered and available, I have a bunch of transmissions which is basically notes about symbols. Each transmission could be a book, they say. To expedite the delivery, I am providing a short version of the concepts in this third book, To Stop Extinction.

You may wonder: if the off-world community can put an end to human suffering, why wouldn't they just do so? That is why you are reading this. First, that was tried before and didn't work. It's before the history in our books, but I was there. Humans didn't change. This time, I am one of the boats coming for people on their roof during the flood. I'm probably not what you expected nor hoped for, but here I am, nonetheless.

So, here is a quick fix which we will go into detail about in the Foundation. With these 7 words, 3 steps you take with your mind, you save the world:

Be sincere.

Be honest.

Support Human Rights.

For example, if everyone used these 7 words as their guide, what problem is not corrected? It's not that difficult of a concept. The challenge is in personal conversion and application, i.e., believing it and doing it. As with all activations, we must implement a process with a large enough group of people to achieve manifestation. This is detailed in Part 2 of this book.

Humans must show that they want to continue as a species. Why would the off-world community save humans if humans are not interested in saving themselves? Please, give yourself a better future, take a small leap even if you're not sure, allow us to show you that off-world we are sincere and honest.

Each of you are invited to participate in projects about which you feel strongly. Your passion can be stronger than anything on this earth. Let us show you how.

I could have a fancy hard-wired communication bridge to off-world: a portal. That would be great. I know how it is done. But I'm on a tight budget, so I have a sort of ET phone home set up, it works now and then, intermittent with a bunch of distortion.

And off-world distortion isn't just fuzzy reception, we're not talking about puny radio waves anymore.

With my comm bridge I can provide proof on your terms. I can get you 30 minutes of un-diluted truth which can change everything for you. Proof on your terms. You decide: what would it take to prove it to you? You can ask the off-world operatives when I get you connected, and this provides the proof on your terms.

It would be nice if someone wanted to open a portal to the galaxy. I have listed all the tech we can get, probably worth trillions in this economy.

So, if anyone reads this, there you have it. I brought the best, coolest symbols and probable realities to earth.

Thank you for giving us your time and consideration even if you decide against stopping extinction.

If you decide to save humans, sign up and participate, make a ten-minute investment in the fate of humanity.

Tom

Christmas Eve, 2022

The 5000 Year Message

This world is an illusion,

I am immortal and will live many lives,

My desire creates my suffering,

I forgive those who trespass against me.

The Source

Lao-Tze's message: what is, is not. The world is an illusion

Krishna's message: you are immortal and will live many lives

Buddha's message: desire creates suffering

Jesus' message: forgive those who trespass against you

Interpretation

Here is a simple interpretation of each part of the message.

The world is an illusion.

As we experience it, physical reality is real. You can put a rock in a box and 50 years from now, it will be the same. This picture is created with our 5 senses, and we can all agree, today is a date, there is a time, the mountains are old, my house is the same color every day, food has a flavor, flowers have a scent, the sky is blue, etc.

But the definition we are missing is that what is real does not change. In this world, in this universe, what does not change? Well, everything changes. So, from a greater perspective, everything in the physical world is temporary.

Who has this perspective which sees a billion years as easily as a moment? The one who designed this reality and created time. What is real from that perspective is that which does not change. Everything else is illusion. And this is true.

In my experience, after living 600 lifetimes, I can say that without exception, when I went back to my home a thousand years ago, it was gone, the village or town I lived in was gone. There might have been some fragments of this or that, but that is not my beautiful house. Everything was temporary in this world. However, in the next realm, off-world, it all still exists.

The purpose of this knowledge that the world is an illusion is to keep your cool. If you found yourself in a place you knew wasn't real, how would you act differently than you act now?

We may start to understand that what we are reacting to is only an incitement, a trigger to make us react.

So, what is your reaction? The idea is to look at your reaction. In the moment, you may just react. But afterwards, look at why you reacted.

Just as important, what is your response? When you have a reaction, how do you respond, what do you do? So, our reaction and response gives us insight into who we are.

This doesn't mean you shouldn't be passionate; it means you should be passionate. Your emotions are real, they will exist after this life is over, after your beautiful house is gone. Your emotions are more real than your house. Your house may be gone in a couple hundred years, though it doesn't matter because it will be gone from you the day you die, which will be quicker than a couple hundred years. Now, when you dies and a couple hundred years from now, you will still have the same feelings for your house. Your feelings are real, the house relatively temporary.

I am immortal and will live many lifetimes.

In this moment, I must say I am sorry that Lord Krisna's message has been confused by his many beautiful quotations. Lord Krishna's message I present may seem an obvious truth of the Hindu religion. The message from Lord Krisna I present here is the message which is his contribution to these four messages which are so critical to understanding our world. The 5000-Year Message would not be what it is without inclusion of the Hindu contribution.

Many people I see would like to live forever.

Congratulations, you will.

5

I know, they want to be themselves forever in this life they are living. No matter how nice your life is, the truth is better than that.

My life on earth is beset with all kinds of maintenance, problems, issues and setbacks, people around me feeling bad, being treated badly, you name it. We leave the bad bits and keep the good bits.

This doesn't mean your lifetimes go on forever. They don't. My off-world survey is that the average soul lives 200-300 lifetimes before they are done with this world. Some quit after 1 lifetime, some go over 1000 lifetimes. Your choice.

The purpose of this message is to put you at peace. Even though you will walk through the door of passing alone, you will not stop existing, you will live forever, you are not alone. Don't fret about life getting away from you. If you want to live again, you will, as many times as your like.

Many people believe that their soul will leave their body upon death, after the last breath. But isn't the flip side just as obvious: your soul entered your body at birth, upon the first breath. The true story has been hidden from you. If you look at history closely, you will see when and how the truth was taken.

My desire creates my suffering

At some point, we all ask why we must suffer?

You may pass this off to your God who is putting you through all you go through, and hope that it will be explained when this life is over.

At some point, you desired something. If you got it, there may have been a price you didn't see- future suffering.

If you haven't gotten it yet, any suffering related to it is caused by your desire.

The purpose is to really think about what you want. The purpose of this message is to understand the pain you give yourself.

Forgive those who trespass against you

This is the toughest, and it was shown in the toughest way for that reason.

To forgive those who tortured you to death, that's a big step.

Some of us unfortunately may be tortured to death as well, but most of the trespasses are not so serious, and will not have such consequence.

But we all know when something is not right or fair.

In each event, they don't know what they are doing, or they wouldn't do it.

This is not to say they are not intentional in their desire to cause harm. Some are intentional in their desire to cause harm. They know what actions they are taking, and they are purposely taking those actions.

They don't know the ramifications of what they are doing, they may not believe there are ramifications, their emotions may be strong they ignore everything else.

Dozens upon dozens of reasons are used, but the underlying truth is they know what they are doing, but they are ignoring the consequences or don't believe there are consequences.

Perhaps you can forgive those who trespass against you just because you feel it is the right way to be. Good for you.

For others, it helps to know that there will be consequences for anyone who violates the human rights of another human. There will be significant consequences.   The   consequences   must   be significant enough that the person who did the harm experiences the harm they did.

The purpose of this is to give you the most important gift: a way to deal with the pain you experience from the actions of others.

Review

The world is an illusion in which I have put myself. It is beautiful and ugly, exciting and boring, pleasant and thrilling, painful and frustrating. After everyone I know is gone, my world is gone. My experience, what I feel and think is real, but this place was only real for me for a period of time.

My existence is not limited to this life. I will live on forever. I can live again as many times as I want.

It is natural I have desires, things that I want. But these adventures can cause me suffering if I don't I get what I want, and some actions can cause me suffering because I got what I wanted.

In all these experiences, there are those who will trespass against you. As you have suffered, know that they create an inevitable suffering for themselves by trespassing. Forgive them instead of carrying the weight of emotions which bind you to someone you want nothing to do with.

This message has been available for a couple thousand years but has not been widely reconstructed. In simple words, the message provides human beings with the concept behind the design of human beings from the designer.

In the last 5000 years, there have been 4 scenarios Christ directly entered humans, so Christ could speak directly to each of us. This message has been given in 4 parts over the course of thousands of years.

Each time the designer of our world spoke through a person, there was a different, single, short message.

After each line, stop and think a bit about what it means.

This is a simple guide to being a human on this planet, from the designer.

Foundation

In each Off-World book, the same Foundation is included as part of the appendix which is called Setting the Table.

The Foundation contains foundational information which we feel is needed to understand an Off-World book.

7 Words

With the book The 5000 Year Message, we are given a guide to being human by the designer. In about 25 words. It was started 5000 years ago and arrived this year for you. It is a way to help you understand your experience as a human.

You can say it is not possible, but it is.

You can say you don't believe it, but you will.

Now, from the same source, at the 11th hour, we are given maybe 7 words on how we each can save the world. In 3 small steps. That would be awesome if I could take credit for the 7 Words solution, but that would be presumptuous.

14 years ago, I told the story of a woman who did something unusual. And one day, I asked her why, and she said, "it's something beautiful...that I can do." She didn't feel she had anything to offer the world, but this was something beautiful that she could do.

Now it's your turn. On this foundation, we save the world. But it's not me, it's you. It's you who saves the world. With 3 small steps, maybe 7 words.

Our Foundation is that 7 words will save the world. If earth is saved from extinction, the concepts of these 7 words will be in the mindset whether this program is known or not known.

You can take these 3 small steps. At home, sitting at your kitchen table, you can do your bit to save the world. And all you must do is take 3 small steps...with your mind.

Don't make it more difficult than this because it's not. The rest will follow because it has no choice but to follow. You will be compelling because of 3 steps you have taken with your mind. You will be a magnet which draws balance to the world. Maybe not today or tomorrow, but over the course of the next decades.

You may think I'm just saying words, making stuff up. But in time, you will look back and know that you saved the world, because saving the world for you can only be what you can do. You can't do more than what you can do. You are not being asked to do more than you can do.

But you don't know what to do to save the world. You feel there is nothing you can do to save the world. But that's not true, you can do this to save the world.

My part is to tell you that you will look back and know someday that you did the right thing, and it did matter. It made all the difference, even though you couldn't see it at the time.

You don't have to see all of that, you just have to look at yourself and that's enough. Your task has always been to make you your best self. And this is how you can do it. And you can feel good about yourself for this reason. In your mind, you know that you did the right thing.

You will stumble, you're human, but if you give yourself a simple understanding, you will always be able to get back on your path. This is something beautiful that you can do. Right here, right now. And with this beauty you create, because you decided to do it, if you don't the part you would play will not be played.

You don't have to tell anyone that you have made this decision, but you can tell whomever you like.

Perhaps this is just a book, and these words are just a bit of ink on paper. But, perhaps, this is message sent to you personally.

You really want to, but the world is so filled with hurt, we stay where we are safe if we can find that place. And we all wonder, can't this world be better?

All that causes pain in the world has it's time and is over and turns to dust. But that which is real lasts. And you are here to do something real when it really matters.

Step 1: Be sincere.

Step 2: Be honest.

Step 3: Support human rights.

That's it. Seven words. Three steps. And you have done your part. What these steps mean to you will unfold as you live your life. In every interaction, you take 3 steps with your mind.

How can this save the world?

Because, if everyone does it, what problem still exists in the world? What is the problem which comes to your mind? Is it not solved for any group of people who take these steps?

And if you want a next step to solve the problem which comes to your mind, if you understand how that problems can be solved with a simple solution, then your decisions follow. So, 7 words are not the solution, 7 words are presented here as a way to understand a basis for making decisions before you think, speak and act.

But not everyone will do this.

Not today, but over time groups of people will, and they will come to act together. Every person who sees the problem that you see wants a simple solution. Like magnets drawn together, and magnets pushing away from those who don't want to save the world.

Some will be taking these 3 steps even if they never read these words, and they will save the world, because they will do what they can do, no more is asked and no more is required.

Step 1: Be Sincere

Being sincere means being authentic, by speaking your truth based on how you feel, what you think and believe. You don't have to add emotion because you feel that is the only way to be heard. If you act with sincerity, you already have more power than you may feel.

Step 2: Be Honest

Being honest does not mean saying bad things and things that hurt. It simply means not saying something false. Many different emotions from love and fear can generate reaction and response. If a response is hurtful and the truth is beautiful, then that response is not the entire story, it is part of the pain. You don't really want to be a purveyor of pain.

If the question violates you right to privacy, then you don't answer it with that reason: that is personal. Or simply: I don't have to answer that.

Being honest means telling the truth when it is important to tell the truth: when someone else is not telling the truth. The truth at that moment is: the other person is not telling the truth. You may not know what the truth is or may not be able to think of it at any given moment, all you have to know is that the truth is beautiful and the other person is only telling a half-truth or something which is false.

Step 3: Support Human Rights

Supporting human rights is the big challenge for many people. We support our human rights, but can we support the human rights of others?

By supporting human rights of others, it is included that our human rights are supported, too. We support these human rights for everyone.

While so many claim their rights are violated, what rights are these?

These human rights are provided and explained in the book A Definition of Human Rights. To support human rights, you must know what human rights are, all your human rights. We have a list, it's just a list, but it's a pretty good list.

It doesn't matter where you are if you can shut out the world for a couple minutes. But maybe make a note of where you are, for this is where and when you decided to save the world. That is a big decision. For each step, you think about it for a few seconds, understand what it means, and decide in your mind. Whenever you don't know what to do, review your choices with the 3 steps as your understanding.

I will be sincere.

I will be honest.

I will support human rights.

That's it. You did it.

Activation

Most people must deal with the world. We must get to work in the morning. This is part of what they want to help us change. This is your quality of life tapping on your shoulder. You see, the two-stage concept of this projection is that by fixing stuff for humans, humans can fix stuff for earth. This is a bold wager, off-world, heads are shaking: if we give humans a better life, they will stop hurting each other and repair earth. Like we say, 30% chance on a good day.

And, as ridiculous as it sounds, they assert to me that all we must do is care. But in this case, caring means being sincere and honest and supporting human rights. It's not just "I care", it's "Because I care, I'm sincere and honest and I support human rights."

How does that work? There are a few little tasks you can do if you care, but they are not that big. We can do these tasks while we sit at the kitchen table. Less than ten minutes, but even if you want to do more, it's less than hour a month while at home. If you choose to do something, it's ok even if you can only handle the smallest of somethings. Everyone is welcome, if you are human, you are needed.

Activation is the process of making change occur in the physical world, here on earth.

So, activation is the important step which sets change in motion. If a large enough group of people want something good, the change is initiated.

How to do this is mysterious to most people. Off-World, we see exactly how it takes place. Unfortunately, most of these activations are not for making the world a better place. So, we want to activate. We will do this for specific reasons at specific times with specific actions.

So, sign up with us so we can activate you when the time is right. We do not call to sell you something or talk you into something. We can text you or email you when an action is needed. We will provide you with what to do, which usually will not take more than ten minutes. You will not have to convince anyone of anything. It is that easy. Because we know how this works, we can make something happen if enough people sign up to allocate ten minutes of their time. We need about a million people to want to save the world. It takes place in small actions by you. No one will make you do something you don't want to do, that's not how we change the world.

We need a million and there are 8 billion on earth. So, we need one of ten thousand humans to give 5 minutes a month to save themselves and 10,000 more humans, people they don't know. I know, it's a hard sell, no takers yet.

The List of Human Rights

Each human right on the list is explained in the book A Definition of Human Rights:

1. A human being has the right to safety
2. A human being has the right to protection
3. A human being has the right to eat
4. A human being has the right to land
5. A human being has the right to home
6. A human being has the right to education
7. A human being has the right to own
8. A human being has the right to work
9. A human being has the right to commerce
10. A human being has the right to travel
11. A human being has the right to family
12. A human being has the right to tribe
13. A human being has the right to retire
14. A human being has the right to care
15. A human being has the right to equality
16. A human being has the right of dominion
17. A human being has the right to privacy
18. A human being has the right to truth
19. A human being has the right to think
20. A human being has the right to expression

21. A human being has the right to preference
22. A human being has the right to understand
23. A human being has children's rights when they are a child.
24. A human being has parent's rights when they are a parent of a child.
25. A human being has legal rights

The Off-World Community

There are 8 billion or so people living on earth. If you are not one of these, you are off-world, world meaning earth. Anyone who is not a breathing human is part of what I am calling the off-world community.

There is an illusion of separation between humans on earth and the off-world community. This illusion of separation only applies to humans, and not to the off-world community.

While people don't generally associate beings from other planets and people whose life has ended, entities or archangels, and Christ, this is because they don't understand the nature of the off-world community.

I do. Though my access is primitive and limited while I'm breathing, I can make it work.

For example, when I am off-world and meet someone I knew whose life has ended, it is common for them to be perplexed and ask me, "How is it you can be here (in heaven), you're not

24

supposed to be able to do this. How is it you can see me and talk to me?"

If humans understood the nature of physical reality and the nature of time, then it would be understood that the off-world community is right here with you, your senses do not detect the off-world community. This is by design. I understand the framework, which is the structure of this construction.

Summary

There are 8 billion humans living and breathing in the earthly community.

Everyone else is part of the off-world community.

We are part of the off-world community and offer contact.

We offer to save humans from extinction.

Our chosen method is significant improvement in the quality of human lives.

We offer to repair earth.

Our chosen method is to save earth from humanity without harm to humans.

We are using this method of working with a liaison to avoid global trauma and chaos.

The Design of This Universe

While these names God and Christ are not used much off-world, it is important to Christian Americans to acknowledge God as the one who created the universe and all the souls in it. And this is true. Off-world, a different description of God is used.

In the off-world community, these names and descriptions are part of accurate and comprehensive symbols. Here on earth, they are names in a language. As a human on earth, I understand the off-world descriptions may be too ambiguous to be useful to some humans.

God

The first name is God. We can use the name God for the totality of the universe. It should be obvious that the universe was created, for nothing has ever created itself. It would be honest to say you didn't know who created the universe if you don't, but to assert that no one created the universe exposes an emotional motivation. There is no evidence that anything created itself, let alone the universe. Without additional definition of God, we can simply say God is a name for the creator of the universe.

In the off-world community, God is named more like a concept meaning All That Exists or All There Is, which is a concept of unity. In other words, off-world we know the universe is living and conscious, even though it is not focused into a personality such as humans have when alive on earth.

If you have consciousness and awareness that you are part of a whole, and cannot be separated, then you understand a cohesiveness. If your hand told you that it was separate from you, you wouldn't take it seriously, it's part of you.

The reason God as a term is not used so much off-world is because God connotates a human personality, typically a father figure. While this is not technically accurate, it's a symbol like any other. Obviously, a human person couldn't contain the entire universe, but some personify God as a human, and all humans have a right to believe as they choose.

The basic mistranslation or error in translation which was communicated a few thousand years ago was that man was created in God's image. The intended meaning was lost. The intended meaning was that man was created in an image of Gods. This means an image God had or God imagined man.

In linguistics, translation of possessive pronouns and prepositional phrases is painfully difficult, no more than here.

I'm not sure of the delineation in design, but it is generally understood that God and Christ are the designer of humans. We reference the designer of humans as the designer. Off-world there are archangels or entities who were part of the project. When this life is over for you, you will be able to access the archives on these records, and for validation you will be able to interview these beings on the project to acquires resolution for any aspects you do not understand.

Christ

The second significant name is Christ. Off-world, the symbol for the designer of humans means something like the word messiah. The messiah has his own realm of which we and all in this world are part of. This is the lower half of the universe, starting with the physical and moving through what some call the realms of heaven. We have tried to provide a good and easy metaphor later in this Foundation in the section A Way to See the World.

Now, in colloquial terms, you can call this consciousness Christ, the son of God. It's not precisely accurate, but it creates a human description, one that we can understand. It's ok, I think. Now, the word Christ originally meant something like vessel or container, it's been a couple thousand years since I spoke Ancient Greek well, so I've given up trying to remember. So, Jesus was a man who became the vessel or Christ for the son of God. Over time, we have come to simply call the son of God Christ. So, this is workable, even though it is a small fragment of the true story. We could provide Christians with significant details of that story, but our observation is that when you are stubborn, you are not looking for information, you are avoiding information. So, in these transmissions, we will refer to the consciousness of the messiah plane, which contains heaven and earth, sometimes as Christ, but more often as the designer.

On earth, naming is important to many people. While off-world, a meaning can be conveyed as easily as a name, and so a meaning is preferred. We will use names for clarity. We understand because many believe these figures exist and some don't believe. This disagreement is used to create a significant illusion of separation between these peoples. Your choice is to participate in this illusion of separation or not.

For clarity, it is true that there is what you call a God and Christ, and that this universe was created. Just because science doesn't understand the mechanics of this construction does not mean it constructed itself. That is silly, nothing constructs itself, anything created is created from a greater place. That the design and construction details and drawings are not available to you is by intention.

The designation of Christ as the son of God utilizes human patriarchy, so is inaccurate, but conveys the concept that the Messiah is under God, a part of God. In these transmissions, the Messiah or Christ is often referred to as the designer: the designer of the world and humans and all living creatures.

Christ Events

As is described in the transmission The 5000-Year Message, the messiah can speak through any human the messiah chooses, the messiah is the medium or etheric field in which human bodies exist, ensouled by a soul. In other words, our world and everything in it is part of Christ, so any action is possible by Christ. These actions may be called miracles. This characterization is due to the lack of understanding of the technology applied to a pre-existing structure.

For ease of communication and avoiding conflict, we can call these events Christ Events. Because Christian texts only reference the period of 1000 B.C. to 0 A.D. in the area called the middle east, there is only documentation of one Christ event, and the documentation includes only a small portion of the event.

As best can be discerned through off-world archival review, Christ Events are of two types.

The first type of Christ Event is when a human species upgrade is actuated. It is common knowledge off-world that this has happened at least a dozen times in the last 7 million years. Some are upgrades, some are tangential variations. A couple examples of these variations known in the western world are a bigger version perhaps double the size of other versions and a long-lived version which lived several times the human lifetime. Each of these variations had their own conceptual purpose. The most recent upgrades, which is comparatively well-documented, is the upgrade from Neanderthal to Homo Sapiens. This took place over 40,000 years ago. The story of the middle eastern part of this event has survived as the story of Adam and Eve in the Old Testament.

It should be noted that there were more than Adam and Eve who received the upgrade in the middle east, so that the species could reproduce. The designer placed a failsafe in the DNA where family members cannot reproduce successfully in one of four such reproductions. So, because of this failsafe, either the new species would be immediately mixed with the prior species for reproduction, or if familial reproduction would immediately result in significant degradation of the new species. The simple solution the designer used was that more than Adam and Eve were upgraded so that the new species could reproduce, though this information is not included in surviving texts.

It should be noted that there were not one set of Adam and Eve, but five sets. These created the five races. The designer's five original races were Caucasian in the middle east, black in Africa, red in Atlantis, brown or Polynesian in Mu, and Asian in

Asia. These races have been mixed in the ensuing millennia, especially recently. Of special importance is that the main basis of conflict in America is this original difference introduced by the designer. One can see that the overcoming of this difference is the test of humans. If this is overcome, we can be embraced by the galaxy. America, in this application, serves as the meeting place of the five races and the battleground for this concept. Will fear or love prevail? This will be a precursor to extinction, or the resolution of the conflict. We are here to promote resolution of the conflict. It should be noted that those who promote the conflict are also promoting extinction. This can be witnessed in their common awareness of an event called the rapture. Proper translation of this concept from the off-world symbol based on the meaning would be extinction, not rapture. The return of souls to heaven, or home, when a life is over or ended is given and always true. This cannot be altered by the concepts and beliefs of humans, this is part of the design; this is how it works.

The first type of event is physical, an improvement to the design of the species. The second type of event is psychological. These events have taken place since the last physical upgrade to homo sapiens. The reason is that prior to this physical upgrade, the human species did not include a critical thinking ability, and as a result did not have more than simple tribal organization. Tribes prior to homo sapiens did not get much larger than 150 humans.

The second type of event is when a concept is presented which is intended to improve the understanding of humans. In the Free Will Model which will be described in one of the next sections, the human design includes free will as part of the design specification. As a counterbalance to free will, which generally results in significant conflict, the designer has initiated this second type of event which seeks to pacify the destructive inclinations of humans operating from fear.

Love and fear can be seen as opposites, hate simply being the state of unable to love. Love can be understood to be a human form of truth. The simplest description of love for humans we have is that love can be seen as manifesting in four actions: respecting, appreciating, giving, and receiving. There are many perspectives off-world, and this is true for love as well, so we present this definition which we see as the simplest. Fear is used by humans as the basis for all acts which are in violation of human rights. Therefore, the most important condition for off-world participation is support of human rights. See the transmission A Definition of Human Rights for a thorough list and explanation of human rights.

This second type of event has taken place four times in the last 5000 years. The compilation of the meaning from these four events is provided in the transmission The 5000-Year Message.

There is always agreement by the souls involved to allow this second type of event, psychological events. There have been approximately 30 such events and agreements, usually with more than one soul participating, usually taking place over a period of more than 50 years.

Jesus

We will speak a bit about Jesus as we knew him because there is so much energy from American Christians who want to know. From our experience in heaven, it is not that people want to know about Jesus. For many, often the most startling and painful knowledge is that Jesus did not want followers and did not offer forgiveness to those who accepted him as their savior. That forgiveness was already inherent in being born and came from the designer. So, Jesus, being sincere and honest, would never act as though a power was his which was not his power. Forgiveness is automatic, restitution must still be made for violations of others' human rights.

Jesus was a man. He was a remarkably interesting man, but I am still challenged to understand Christian's adulation of him. Because he was nothing like his American followers. Jesus has moved forward to a larger existence, which he earned.

If you want to know what he looked like generally, just go to a mosque or synagogue and pick out a tall, middle eastern fellow of average build with a beard and long hair, about 30 years old, if such a person exists.

Jesus did not want a church. Jesus never had a church.

Jesus accepted that a religion would be generated from the designer event.

His message came from the designer. The designer selected Jesus because he was the best messenger for the message of the event which was forgiveness. However, the message was forgiveness of others who trespass against you, not forgiveness of you if you accept him as your savior.

Your relationship with Jesus and the designer existed before you were born and is not changed by any belief you choose in your human life. You have a much larger relationship with the designer than can take place in any lifetime.

Jesus' message came from the designer. In A Way to See the World, we present that your beliefs, and thoughts and feelings and actions create an energy. The resonance of this energy does not exist solely in our minds, this energy resonates off-world, which means it resonates with the designer.

This was true for Jesus as well. In this way, Jesus resonated with the designer better than any other human at the time in the chosen location. Jesus was therefore the best man to project the designer's fourth message, the message of forgiveness.

There has been a formation of church and members who have decided this means if you accept Jesus you are forgiven. There is truth in this, but mainly it is incorrect, and it is not the designer's message through Jesus.

The message was to forgive others who trespass against you.

We have provided a modern detail of this meaning. This is support of human rights, yours and everyone else. Those who trespass against you violate your human rights. When you trespass against others, you violate their human rights. Support of human rights is the same as not trespassing but provides a clearer and more detailed description of what it means to not trespass. This detailed description is provided in A Definition of Human Rights.

If you don't like someone, or something they have done, your task is to forgive them. That you forgive them is not required for forgiveness, that you accept Jesus Christ as your savior is not required for forgiveness, you are already forgiven for the trespasses you have done and will do in the future. To repeat this specifically: you are already forgiven as a birthright, you do not need to ask for forgiveness, you do not need to accept Jesus or anyone as your savior for forgiveness. To accept Jesus as your savior may elicit a change in your behavior as is your choice, but the act of acceptance as your savior does not in itself grant you anything, and Jesus did not want you to accept him as your savior. Constantine make this up in the fourth century to get Christians to bow down to him the way Romans bowed down to him as Caesar.

The part left out is that restitution will be required for the violation of the human rights of others. When the lord says vengeance is mine, this means that you are not the one who extracts vengeance. Violations of the human rights of others incurs debt, or karma, and will require restitution at the time of your choosing. It is equally difficult to resist vengeance. This the fourth of the designer's messages because it is the most important and the most difficult. If you support human rights, then you do not violate human rights with vengeance.

That you will be forgiven is inherent. You do not have to accept Jesus or Christ to be forgiven. How is it you think you can speak for the designer of humans and decide who is forgiven? The designer already forgave you before you trespassed. How is it you think the designer is bound by time? The designer created our experience of time as moments and experiences it all at once, continuously.

As presented in A Way to See the World, Christ is the world we live in, Christ is the recorder of thoughts and feelings and beliefs and actions. The body you inhabit is Christ's work, you cannot exist at any point where you are not using the world he designed. There is no price for this, it's a gift, do with it as you please. However, the designer is not responsible for your choices. One purpose of being human is to understand that you can choose who you become.

It's hard for us to understand the world this way. It is somehow easier to see Christ as the ocean, and we are the bottles of water in the ocean. The ocean and the bottles and the water are all Christ's design and invention.

Now, some have trauma which is the result of a violation of their rights, and their behavior is a response to that trauma. When that behavior violates the rights of other, they will still incur debt. Now, it would be much better if you did not violate the rights of another, if you can control yourself. No one ever plans to incur debt in a life, the incurring of debt always causes one pain, and the restitution much more pain.

This does not mean you have to enjoy what you do not enjoy. This does not mean you should be happy when you are sad. This does not mean you should love yourself when you cannot. This does not mean you should not scream when you are angry. Though if you scream at others or in their presence, they may not want to associate with you, and that is simply exerting their right to preference.

It does mean that even though it doesn't feel like it, in the ways that matter, you are never alone.

The Logic of the Construction of the Universe

This is a simple 4 step progression of logic we apply, which we call The Logic of Construction of the Universe. While this is a simple symbol off-world, we cannot think of more concise wording. The Logic of the Construction of the Universe is subject to your review:

1. Nothing creates itself, therefore the universe was .created
2. If the universe was created, there must be a design for the universe which set the rules by which the universe exists.
3. You do not have these design details and drawings, the one who has the design details and drawings has not given them to you.
4. It must be the intention of the designer that you are not overtly given the design details and drawings.

For clarity, and as a comfort to self-proclaimed atheists, it is true that God is not a guy in a robe with a long beard. It is also true that God and Christ are not humans sitting on clouds to whom you will sit next to for eternity. In this situation, your assertion is correct that God and Christ cannot be human or human-like, especially the two characteristics of being Caucasian males.

For those who understand this, your expectation that others would be able to grow beyond this concept is obviously in error. The error in this case is yours if your expectation of others is based on your understanding or beliefs. In other words, because you have a larger understanding of the universe does not mean others are capable of this larger understanding of truth. The larger understanding is that a human could not have created the universe. You benefit from this awareness; it is worth giving yourself credit for reaching this comprehension.

It is important to understand that we each have a right to belief, and those beliefs define a state we experience. This experience of the manifestation of a life derived from beliefs and thoughts and feelings is the purpose of your life and all human lives.

Your denial of what you know is logical due to your feelings is your right. The next step after this denial is to want to know and to understand. Typically, there is an anger or frustration that is if a larger design is correct, it should somehow be conveyed to you. The purpose of the Logic of the Construction of the Universe is to offer you understanding without any attached descriptions. A state of denial is just the starting position in the progression you experience. You can refuse to listen and think for as long as you like, and a great portion of humans do just that.

After our lives are over, we will look back and want to know what was true and what was a mistake. This may take a century for those who strongly refuse to think or listen, because everyone has a right to do as they choose. In all these choices, there was an overriding emotion which compelled a person to do what they did, and that is the learning.

We say the next step because you are not alone in this state, it is shared by many, and for most the next step is to want to know. We can assist in this, but you would have to be able to conclude in your own mind that you want to know and change from a state of denial. You cannot and will not be forced to change, the right of free will inherently include the right to be in error, that is the purpose of free will: to enable you and give you the right to be in error and experience the result of that error personally.

Meet and Greet in Heaven

In closing, let me try this. I work with a group, and all of us who do this work can tell stories of people whose body has died, and they won't even listen to their mom or dad or spouse because they know and believe completely that Jesus is going to meet them when they pass over, or Christ, or God, or Moses, or we don't know who, their third-grade teacher. So, anything else is a trick, most commonly a trick of the devil.

Every perspective has a price, and for so many perspectives the price is higher than I am willing to pay any more, i.e., I'm too old for this. I sigh a big sigh before I dive in to help such a poor soul, the price and restitution of my own perspective long ago. How many more payments have I got to go?

"Ok, guys," I say to the team, "who is going to play Jesus this time so this poor soul will listen to the truth." Jesus has moved way past meet and greet at the pearly gates. Don't you think he earned it?

Great, it is my turn. The hard part if figuring out what the poor soul expects Jesus to look like. And then I find out they are not expecting Jesus at all, they believe they are not worthy of Jesus' attention. Great. And what the poor soul doesn't know is that the truth is much better than what they believe and fear, the truth is infinitely better, unbelievably better. The benefit of the truth to them personally is incredible. But they have a whole bunch of fear, and their fear resulted in a very stubborn inaccurate belief.

If only we can get them to listen. And they sit there, hands over their ears, eyes closed, chanting "I am not listening, you're the devil, I know who is coming for me any second. I refuse, I refuse, I refuse. Go away." This can go on for years, so we try for longest time and then just come back later, it may take them a week or a century to calm down. There's no shortage of time, so no big deal. Eventually, one of us figures out how to get the poor soul to listen, he believed that his first pastor when he was a kid would be in heaven to guide him. If we can find the pastor, our work is done. Just another fun time off-world.

Summary

There are two significant names with regards to the design of the universe.

The first is God and the second is Christ.

God created the universe.

Christ designed humans and all other life.

God and Christ are not human, nor like a human.

Christ Events are when Christ uses a human to provide guidance or understanding to humans or when a species upgrade is done.

For example, Christ used Jesus to provide a guidance to humans: forgive others who trespass against you.

A Way to Understand the World

There is a way to see the world, which I hope will add clarity. You may have heard of this metaphor; a few teachers tell variations.

So, there is an ocean. In the ocean there are bottles of water.

Each bottle is a person. It appears to each person that they are separate from all the other bottles, and it appears they are in the ocean but not part of the ocean.

This ocean of water is the field we find ourselves in. By field, I mean an etheric field. All space is like an ocean which is a conscious, aware, listening, observing, an active part of the designer. In this model, the world we live in is an imagining of the designer, with all of us and all our stuff.

The field is not just conscious, the designer created the field and is the field. The designer created the ocean, the water, and the bottles. We arrive as souls in this neighborhood of the galaxy to participate in what the designer offers. And when we first see earth, it is Disneyland times a million, we cannot believe it. We cannot believe our luck because it is free for us to use. This is not a task of making something and walking away, the field is a part of the designer. The designer is not separate from the physical world, the designer is the physical world, and we are part of this. As a soul, we can choose and have our own thoughts and feelings.

The universe is not an accident of elements interacting; it is by design. That you experience separation in your skin and thoughts is not by accident, it is by design. The world we experience is a field which is the designer. Think of it, we come into a body, get to control the body, and live a life. And then it is over. But the entire life is recorded in 3 dimensions complete with all your thoughts and feelings.

Time is even better. You experience time as a linear series of events while you are a bottle. But time is part of the field. Time is part of the design. God created all souls at the time of the big bang. The designer created, designed the world we get to experience. Time is part of the design to create experience.

As they created time, they are the masters of time, they are not part of time, time is one of their tools, one of their inventions. They are not marked by time; they use time to mark. Like a series of notches in a piece of wood. Or beats on a drum. The time does not control the designer, like the notches do not control the one who makes them in the wood. They use the notches to enable you to have experience, they create the seconds and design you to experience each second, one at a time, and have a thought in one second, a hope in another, and an action in another.

We were each created as souls, sparks with a consciousness of our own, so that we could do these things in the field, and the designer beats the drum, and with each beat, we take another step, think another thought, feel another emotion, and then we act.

Our actions are not controlled, our power to choose actions is the purpose of life. We are let loose on the earth. However, each soul who becomes a human has rights. And to ignore these rights means you don't understand the pain your ignorance will cause.

The ramifications of our thoughts, feelings and beliefs and actions are not immediate. But the ramifications are often much more significant that the act. You can kill someone with a thought, a feeling, and an act in a second. Restitution may take you hundreds of years. You will be given all the years you need, take a century, take millennia, but restitution will be made. Someone dies in a second. One second, they are alive, one second, they are dead. But restitution takes all the time in the world.

Will you be forgiven? You were always forgiven. You were never in a state of not being forgiven. Only someone who wanted you to obey them would assert such a threat that you would not be forgiven. Anyone who asserts that you are not forgiven is making up stuff way beyond their pay grade.

But it is simpler than that, if you are forgiven, you have advantage. Only someone who wanted advantage over others would embrace such an idea. So, yes, you will be forgiven. But you still got to do the restitution. Take your time, whenever you are ready.

Where is the mark of our acts? Where is the recording? The mark is in the ocean where we are in our bottles, in the field we call the world and the universe.

This is why there are 3 conditions given: sincerity, honesty, and support of human rights. If you follow these, you will not hurt others. This is the design of the designer.

So, in our ocean, our etheric field, every action is not just an action. Each act works like a spark if the act supports the rights of another. Or has no power or energy if it does not support the rights of others.

Because the ocean is a field, an etheric field, and a unified field, that which exists in every drop, everything is any drop is available to us in every drop. So, string theory is correct, but physicists are looking at the wrong fields, quantum entanglement is a small part of this lacking inherent intelligence. Every particle is connected by design. Even though as humans we are cut off from these connections during our lives. Maybe we think we can feel the connections sometimes, and probably we do.

So, we humans face some challenges. Our design overwhelms us, and we cannot focus. This is part of the design. But that does not mean we are doomed. It is known by the designer, designed by the designer, that we would most likely find ourselves in this situation.

So, what solution does the designer offer? A solution is offered, but it is not the designer stepping in and fixing everything.

The solution to this puzzle is obvious, but you must be sincere.

We fill our ocean with sparks or with darkness.

The ocean contains everything we need- everything which exists is part of the design, and everything which is possible. All the tech, all the environmental solutions, all the social solutions, all the economic solutions.

So, why hasn't someone brought them forward? Solutions are constantly being given, but who will listen?

The things you want may not be here in your living room, but they are connected to you in your living room, even though they may come from light years away, somehow, they are available here and now.

How do we get the solutions which are sitting in your living room? We fill the ocean with sparks or with holes. Sincerity and honesty, we can only do those ourselves. We only got one requirement: supporting the rights of others.

Summary

The designer is like an ocean. In this ocean, there are bottles of water. Humans are the bottles of water. We feel like we are separate from the ocean, but we are part of the ocean.

We experience time as a series of moments, but that is our experience due to our design. The designer does not experience time as we do, the designer is aware of all time and created our experience of time as moments.

You have always been forgiven.

If you violate the human rights of another, there is restitution.

Everything is available to humans. There is no distance between you and all that exists.

Your access to all of this depends on you and all humans.

If you honor the human rights of others, your bottle becomes more transparent, and you increase your participation in the ocean and your access to the ocean.

If you violate the human rights of others, your bottle becomes more opaque, and you decrease you access to the ocean.

Free Will

There is some confusion as to the nature of a free will species. Common Reckoning is something like we have free will or choice. If you belong to a Christian religion, the reckoning may be something like that God gave us free will and will bless us for making good choices.

While this is true, the description is lacking the basis. Off-world, we have access to truth which includes understanding, knowledge, and wisdom. So, there is much less inclination to do things in error, and our ability to do significant damage to anything does not exist.

To design a free will species, understanding, knowledge and wisdom must be blocked. This was done with the design of humans. It sounds difficult, but Christ uses a simple method which works quite well. The mechanism for creating a free will species is that your brain is like an empty hard drive when you are born, you retain no memories or your existence before you were born.

While your consciousness has memories, saving to the hard drive is in temp files for the first couple years of your life, your brain doesn't make strong, permanent memories when you are a baby.

As you live in your body for those first couple years, you start to function only from sensory input and learn how to work the body. Think of it, somehow you, a conscious being, can inhabit and operate this body. How does that work? Obviously, you didn't do it, so someone with a lot more skills did it.

Now, mainly because they are frustrated or stubborn or both, some assert consciousness is inherent to biological life. So, this is backwards. Something is always created from a greater place, nothing creates itself. Consciousness is attached to a being though an incredible designer technology which we will cover in the next section Ensoulment.

When this transition has been made to inhabiting and operating the body in 2-3 years, then you start to make permanent memories. This 2-year period is experienced as something like a dream, you are part of the environment, not in control of the environment.

Now, that's a pretty good design for blocking prior knowledge. And it works most of the time. Your soul still has memories, from a different time as a different person using a different language. I have described in another transmission that this type of perception can be called a symbol. How would that symbol be understood in the mind of child in a different place and time speaking a different language? It would not.

Because we don't have prior memories, we make choices based on our inclinations. This is free will.

Living as a human on earth exposes what we truly believe. That is a pretty good design. It is also a very good example of how meaning is lost living on earth.

Free will is certainly a great gift we were given when we were created as souls, which are self-conscious living beings, immortal and indestructible.

We are not separate from all that exists, souls are a unique type of object in this universe, created at the start. We can't have an experience which is separate from God and Christ, they are the universe, the medium in which we exist, even though with our own consciousness it appears we are separate. While we humans want all being to be human, like us, the power which created a billion galaxies is not human, but instead designed humans as a way to experience the earth.

Once you have some experience in the universe, we know how to behave. To see what you would do if you forgot all you know, we come to earth to have free will. This means we get to make any mistake we are inclined to make.

Someone told us not to murder, for example, but that doesn't stop people from murdering. So, free will is not a freedom per se, it's more like giving yourself amnesia to see if you truly, deeply learned from your experiences or not.

Summary

Humans are a species with free will.

Humans retain no memories from before they were born.

Humans were designed this way.

Humans do as we are inclined to do, without remembering what has happened before. This is how free will is enabled.

Ensoulment

When the universe was created with the Big Bang, all souls were created as well. As was given in the 5000-Year Message, you are an immortal being, a soul.

A soul has consciousness. Your stream of consciousness, the constant thoughts that go through your head is the stream of consciousness of a soul: you.

At the time of birth, with the first breath, the soul is bound to the body.

For a soul, this is one of the designer's best inventions.

How does a soul bind to a body, become the inhabitant and the operator? How does a soul own a body, and become the body?

This is incredible. You can imagine the surprise when souls became aware that the designer had created a technology that enables a soul to inhabit a body.

The process of binding a soul to a body can be called ensoulment. The process of the soul leaving the body can be called desoulment, but we just call it death.

The is a process. We are going from a place where we are a soul in time and space, to a place where we are a human body.

As humans, we have no memory of this process of the binding of our soul to our body. There is no basis for asserting that this process takes place prior to birth. The first breath of life is a good way to view this event. Your soul is attached to the body when the body initially breathes outside the mother.

This is the design of an automated technology we can use but did not make. I compare it to riding a rollercoaster, we can take the ride, but we did not design the ride and do not control the rollercoaster.

You can deny it, you can say you don't believe it, you can fight against the designer's plan, you can scream at God. You can believe with all your being that a body being developed in a womb to be a human is already a human, and this is part of the instincts of other mammals who don't have the ability to think. But this remains the design of ensoulment.

We use this technology to attach to a body and become a human being when a body is ready for birth. This technology is automated, we can use it, but we did not design nor invent it. These technologies that the designer designs are beyond a soul's understanding, which means they are very sophisticated. They don't exist like a machine we can go look at and tinker with.

This design protects a human being from being hurt by the acts of man before we are human beings. This design is smarter than we are. You do not have to protect the unborn, the unborn are not human beings, they are bodies being developed so they can become a human being.

This is not part of your responsibility; you have never been told this is part of your work, and if you were told this, it is not true. The designer of humans is smarter than all humans, his system does not allow acts of humans to destroy the design, the system, and the technology. Even as a soul in heaven, this is beyond our grasp. Have a little confidence that the design for human beings is generally beyond human tampering.

Mother's Instinct

As with all mammals, it is the mother's strongest instinct to keep that developing body safe. The instinct to keep the developing body safe is often stronger than the instinct to survive. That is how species keep going. If the mom didn't care, the species would end there.

And that mother will think of the body as what it will become: a baby. But it is not a baby till it takes that first breath. Instinctively, moms know this, they wait for the first breath, then her work to have a baby is done. When the baby breathes, sometimes with a spank, the human is born into being. It is an important widespread practice now that a baby is held by the mother after birth because it creates that first bond, which moms feel and know instinctively.

In our immediate past, it was common that a mother would not get to hold the baby until a bit later. The point is that the question a mother would ask the nurse is, "Is it all right?" This question is important, it exposes the mother's automatic understanding that while the fetus was developing, preparing to be human, not until the fetus is all right, viable and good on its own, not until then is it a human being.

The body will be owned by a soul and becomes a person when the soul inhabits it with the first breath.

The ensoulment process is not remembered because of the free will design. We do not remember anything before the age of 2 ½. We don't remember being born, and the time prior to birth when we prepared for the big event of our attachment to a physical body. Without any memories, this aspect is just ignored as something without an answer.

Or much worse, people decide that being human starts before birth. Or that a soul is created by a couple people when pregnancy occurs. These ideas are triggered by the instinctive drive. A mother has the instinct to protect a fetus, a developing body. But until the attachment of the soul at birth, and the body breathes, the body is not viable until that moment. The developing body is not a human being, it is being developed. A body is not a human being, when a soul attaches at birth and breathes, that's a human being.

Even then, the soul can decide it is not ready and back out within a few weeks, and this is called sudden infant death syndrome. It doesn't mean anyone did anything wrong, it's not anyone's fault. The soul realized it was not ready to be a human being and left the body.

Energetic Body

The process which takes place in the background is a soul's attachment to the energetic body. The depiction of the energetic body in the second Thor movie was pretty good. Our eyes can't perceive an energetic body, so until recently there was no such thing. We can't see heat, but it exists, but we can feel it. In the past, if we didn't have a sense to sense something, it didn't exist.

This sensory basis ended with radios and medicine more than a century ago. We accept something exists if we get a tangible benefit at the end, we accept we don't understand and cannot sense how it is done, but if there is a tangible result, it must exist. Science overcame the illusion of control that organic reality provided to humans which was: if I can't detect it with my senses, it doesn't exist.

Those who are trained in detecting the energetic body can do some work with the energetic body. If you couldn't see your physical body, then it would be challenging to describe a human body, and this is true with the energetic body and our five senses.

In the Dr. Strange movies, they constantly work with the energetic body. While that is just a movie and what they do with energetic bodies is inaccurate, it is true that we have an energetic body and it is like the energetic bodies in the movie. Just because we haven't given you the technology to view the energetic body yet doesn't mean the technology doesn't exist. But you would have to want the technology, instead of denying the existence of the energetic body and the technology to detect it.

The energetic body is an organization of energy which provides a conduit for the lifeforce. So, this one sentence description has a lot of stuff which doesn't exist for many people, like every word.

An organization of energy is not a concept we have evidence of. Because it is proven and used continuously by us, electricity may be invisible, but we know it is real. When we use the term energy in the phrase organization of energy, we understand the concept of organizing stuff, but we know electricity doesn't work like that. Electricity is electrons which push the next electron which pushes the next electron along wires to a place where it is stored in batteries or used by a device.

When we say organization of energy, what are we talking about? And there's the challenge. Until we completely describe a system, we don't have words to describe it. We haven't made the words up yet. So, with an organization of energy, we immediately go to a place which doesn't exist yet, even though it was in a Thor movie.

If we are talking about electricity as we know it, it isn't organized into forms, it travels on conductive metals when one electron pushes the next electron, and as it does this at the speed of light, we perceive the electricity immediately at the other end of the wire. This is a simple and incomplete description of electricity, which is what we know as energy.

So, is this energy electricity or not? Not. So, first, we are talking about a different type of energy. We use the word energy because it is the only one we have to describe an invisible force which can do things. So, we can qualify this energy as auric energy, relating to an aura. It is not electricity, which is electrons which behave according to laws of science. But if it is not electrons, what is it? What particles are used? These particles are smaller than electrons and quarks, so they are not going to be detectable with our technology.

In the second Thor movie, they have a device with which they can view an energetic body. We don't have this technology yet, but that doesn't mean we can't get it.

This information on the energetic body relates to ensoulment because the energetic body is the system to which our souls can attach. Our soul is connected to the energetic body and the energetic body is connected to the human body.

Think about it for a second, you will leave your body when you die, you are controlling your body right now. How do you control your body right now? Where is the connection between your consciousness and your toes? How does that work? Give yourself the opportunity to understand how this all came about, give yourself the freedom to understand how this all works. All the answers were there, and now a few of those answers are right here for you.

Summary

All souls were created at the time of creation, which can be called the big bang.

You are a soul.

A body is prepared by the mother after she becomes pregnant.

When you are born and take your first breath, your soul attaches to the prepared body.

When you, a soul, attach to a human body at birth, it becomes your body.

This process is one of the designer's technologies and can be called ensoulment. This technology is automated, we did not build it but we can use it.

When you stop breathing, your body dies, and your soul is released from its attachment to your body.

My Part

Liaison

In the movie The Day the Earth Stood Still, the arrival of an alien causes global trauma and chaos. At one point Keanu meets a person at McDonald's who has been embedded on earth. I'm like that fellow, the difference is I'm not an alien, not anymore anyway, but I can act as an Off-World Liaison.

What we want to achieve is saving humanity from extinction and saving earth from humanity, without the global trauma and chaos. Humans hurl undauntedly towards extinction and destruction of earth, generally without concern.

Now, 2/3 of species such as humans destroy their planet and themselves. So pending destruction is not a surprise but a likelihood. At the same time, one-third don't. I am here to help you understand how. Off-world, there is an understanding that humans are in the two-thirds category at the 11th hour.

Humans can be described as an emotionally based, free will species given the right and responsibility for caretaking earth.

Yes, the aliens will come if I call, but I really do not like them. So, because I'm going to need some alien technology for some of these projects, I bit the bullet recently and gave them a call. They showed up within 24 hours, and as I usually do, I ran away, just making sure you guys are still down for the project before I start speaking. I mean, it sounds cool: aliens.

But it's more like dealing with a large lizard or insect or creature, you never know what their game is, but you're pretty sure they don't care about you at all, and it dawns on you they are here for their own reasons, and they have never even heard of my concept of deals and fair play, let alone agreeing to play by my rules. A bit of caution is a good idea.

The good news is that they will give us the tech under the right circumstances, and it doesn't cost us anything. Cost is sort of a human thing, not a universal thing.

I'm sure it seems like fiction, but what I'm going to share is the truth the fictions are based upon. I hope you feel the amazement you felt when you experienced these fictions through reading or in the theater.

Over the last 42,000 years, I have lived about 600 lifetimes on earth. While most finish up in 10,000 years or so, I'm still here. Now that my time here is over, I am one of a few who has been witness to humans moving from first civilizations to this stage, which is either the last stage or a new stage. All I had to do was hang out for forty thousand years.

My interest in earthly life took place after the last upgrade to the species from Neanderthal to Homo Sapiens. These enhancements included some work on the cortex to enable sophisticated mental functions, so it seemed like a good time to jump in.

So, I had the chance to be a part of a new, high-level species on a wilderness planet. What could go wrong?

Perhaps that is a story on its own, but it's not today's story, and for me it was painful enough the first time.

Over the last 10,000 years, about 90 lifetimes, I have developed a special skill set.

There is no title for what I do, so I made up the title Off-World Liaison. I don't know how good of a title it is, but it's the best I could come up with.

Summary

I have access to the Off-World community.

My role is of liaison, facilitator, or broker.

My off-world contacts offer technology and solutions to humans.

These are offered without cost but not without condition.

.

Existential Duality

This is how I do what I do. This is how I do my work as an off-world liaison. I put together into the title of off-world liaison several activities which could also be called multi-dimensional states. What this means is that sometimes I am a human on earth, and sometimes I am not. The term I use for sometimes being a human on earth and sometimes not is Existential Duality.

Most people cannot do this consciously. I do not know if anyone else can do this, until I do what my off-world contacts are telling me we can do together, it hasn't been done, not lately anyway.

Most people cannot be conscious without their body. Some people remember their dreams. Some people even realize they are dreaming sometimes. Beyond that, not much. I've been wondering for most of my life why no one is aware of these experiences.

But for the 9 multi-dimensional states I describe here, I don't know of anyone else who participates like this. I'm sure I can't be the only one. Most humans who can do this just don't come back to being a human again, they're done and on to new horizons.

And don't get me wrong, this is not easy. Try it for yourself. These are the most difficult tasks I know of. Most people who try just give up, it is not possible for them, anyway.

When I am visit heaven while I'm still alive, I get asked every time, "How can you be here? How can you do this?"

When I put in a request to an alien species, they will come, I have some favors I can call in, but I do not like to do it, I don't want to do it, this is not easy stuff, at least not with my skills.

When I work with energetic bodies, I see the cause of conditions. I sometimes get sick, due to the sickness of the energetic body I did work on. They make it look exciting in the movies, but you must know what you are doing, and a lot of the time you're just clueless.

In this healing work, I was working on a woman with chronic pain, specifically in her shoulder. My contacts told me to pass on to her not to call it her shoulder, call it her should-er, she keeps saying in her mind, "I should have…"

So, I got her pain to go away, and that was the first time in a long time, so she was just thrilled for a little relief. Was it in her head? To paraphrase Dumbledore, "Of course it's in your head, just because it's in your head doesn't mean it isn't real."

Someone who does not believe in what I do knew the woman didn't lie, and even though he didn't have a box to put it in, asked me how I did it. I couldn't really answer because I don't really do it, I'm just the tool used by whoever is doing it, I'm just a conduit for energy and truth in that work.

When I work with entities, I always feel like a fool. My concerns and efforts, even to help save the planet, are puny. I've even had entities tell me that those I was asking for help are not really interested. Great.

When I get acquisitions, when I'm given symbols, it's still like being hit with a 2x4 to the head.

When I say I can get you the technology I'm talking about, you need to know I need the energy of many people. And this is not electricity, that's a drop in the bucket compared to the energy I need. The energy I need is maybe a million times stronger than the electricity a city uses. And the tough part is, you don't even know the energy exists. You can't detect it with your eyes and senses.

I'm in the fun position of telling you to help me with your energy. The case to get help is made automatically when activated because those sparks make a big impression. In other words, I need you to activate yourself, and the result is real. But I must help you activate you in the proper way. To that end, they gave me the 3 conditions. This is the simplest way they could figure out to cleanly activate a human.

They say with 3 million properly activated we can do almost anything. We have nearly 300 million in America, so that's 1 in 100. Let us get to it.

So, how do I get there from here. I present the progression in this transmission. Here are the 10 multi-dimensional states as I know them:

1.   Death

2.   Near Death Experience

3.   Lucid Dreaming

4.   Out of Body Experience

5.   Visiting Heaven

6.   Aliens Encounters

7.   Energetic Body

8.   Entities

9.   Acquisition

10.   Bilocation

There are multi-dimensional states with good documentation available, and to these I have added states which have different focuses. The first 4 have quite a bit of documentation, there are books you can read. For the last 6, they represent different focuses. I didn't know I was doing them until they happened, again and again. To accomplish the last 6, it is true you must be able to focus appropriately. This ability is developed over centuries, so if you can do these, you started a long time ago.

People may have not had any of these experiences, so this is just a strange illusion from a mental case...me. As one has these experiences and studies them, the differences between the types of experiences are learned.

I've been studying these experiences for many lifetimes, and I go back and forth between different lifetimes. While time marches on, this is not how I experience it anymore. And when I come back to this life, sometimes I don't know where I am, I may not even know my gender and that can be concerning. It all comes back quickly, and on occasion I've commented, "Who am I?" or "Damn, I'm back here again." Or the scariest, "When in time am I now?"

In the physical world, time marches on, moment by moment. The prior lives are long gone here. When I look for the towns or villages in which I have lived, they are gone. This is when it can dawn on you, the physical world is just a temporary one. It is just like Lao-Tzu said so long ago: it's an illusion.

I still have my prior lives, I still have all those experiences, they are only gone in the mill in which they were churned out, the physical universe.

I still like parts of my last life more than this one, even though I have better skills this time. I can still remember my house I had in Canada, around Banff. I can draw the layout. It had a central grand room of dark wood that is still my favorite room. I remember the color of the drapes and where the hole in the roof was. I ended up there after I went to the Yukon for the gold rush. I did not get much gold, just enough to buy a house and live on. Jack London was there, too, and he wrote a book about these skills. But you don't have to go to prison to do it, that just made sense to him because you must shut out this world for a continuous period of time.

The physical universe creates these realities to the beat of a drum: time. But when you look at time not as a series of seconds, but as a series of centuries, your perception of time and the physical universe changes. I see the universe churning out these sets of experiences, but when one is done, the next starts. When that is done, the next starts. Pretty soon, I have all these sets of experiences we would call lifetimes. But when you step back, they stop being linear, and are more like rows.

As you comprehend the symbols within the lives, you see that the symbols have connection to other symbols. For example, this is not that difficult to understand, in one life I was a son, in another life I had a son, in another life I lost a son, in another life I adopted a son. Son is the symbol. Son exists as a group of thoughts and emotions.

The physical aspect was experienced and ended. The sensory record still exists if you want to experience any part of it again. But the energy is thought and emotion, and it is observable and quantifiable if you have the ability. Every thought and emotion which is part of son. These thoughts and emotions are everything which I felt and thought.

So, not a sentimental parade. Anger, frustration, and pain are as common as love. But in the energetic realm, you see the stronger energy, exponentially stronger, is the love. And just like in the physical universe, the definition of love is not singular. The definition I have appreciated, and use is where love can be seen as 4 actions: giving, receiving, respecting, and appreciating.

The connections are automatic, but you must discern them. This is your purpose between lives. For most of us in most of our lifetimes, this is how we learn, after the life is over, we go over it all and figure out what the hell happened.

But you cannot experience time as a series of centuries while being subject to the beat of time's drum, second by second. With time beating like a drum, you still have your own drumbeat: your beating heart. With every beat of your heart, your body flashes a group of sensory inputs accompanied by a thought or feeling , your stream of consciousness while you simultaneously perceive the world. In this way, you create a movie, a series of flashes equal to your heartbeat.

This is the creation of your experience. With the next beat of your heart, the last sensory flash is replaced by the new flash. While alive we never get to go back; this movie does not have a remote control with pause and rewind. The moments may be saved in our memory, or not.

When you step out of time, that movie stops. When you can look around for a bit without the movie of experiencing your life, you can understand: the drum of time does not beat itself, there is the one who beats the drum, there is the designer who creates time. And the designer of time is not subject to time, they created it for their purposes, but we are subject to time.

One of those purposes is to enable a continuous experience for a soul, you, as a human being. The purpose of this experience as a human being is to experience what it is you experience: your feelings, your thoughts, your beliefs, and your experiences. That's it, that's the purpose of life. You didn't miss it; you are living it. People may want to argue or discuss about the purpose of life, and this is fine, this is one of their purposes.

But one day, and it will happen to all of us, this experience will end. And when you walk through that door, you go through the door alone. Now that sounds scary, and it is. But on the other side of the door of death, everyone you knew who went before is waiting for you, so it's all good.

For most people, this is when the learning starts. When we live a life, we are so focused upon the world we experience and what we must do, and what we want to do, that we do not learn much. We don't know what the experience means, we don't know why we had the experience, we don't know why this or that happened. We had to make a choice and we did, not knowing if it was the right choice or not.

And then the drum beat of time pushes us to the next situation with which we must deal. When this life ends for us, this is when we start learning. It would be nice if we could learn while we are living the life, but usually we are just too busy trying to survive, make our plans happen, and getting through the day. So, we do not.

When you have a physical body and senses, these senses define your world. When you do not have a body and are conscious, you can access a larger universe. It's not a given, but it can be done. The important knowledge is that this is not an unnatural experience. Even more importantly, it's not a illusion. It may seem to be an illusion here, but it's not an illusion where I live, it's my experience.

The perception of this physical universe was designed and created. This perception must be learned, and the initial period of our lives is where we learn this perception, normally our first two years. We learn how to focus upon this reality, and then it is not something which is simply happening to us while we look around, it becomes a place where we can do stuff.

When your heart stops and you stop breathing, that perception ends. It is a forced ending and is experienced as being abrupt. This is the death experience.

There are those whose bodies die, for example, after a heart attack. They are technically dead for a minute or two, and then their heart is restarted. Often, while dead, these people have the same experience as death, which is that they are partially disconnected from their body. When your heart stops and you stop breathing, you will have this experience. When the heart restarts, they breathe again, they re-attach to their body and regain consciousness.

This is called a near-death experience, or NDE. If you don't regain consciousness, it's a death experience. You must die and come back to life to have a near-death experience. There is no guarantee that you will come back, your body may be revived. So, this is not a good method for daily use.

The third type of multi-dimensional experience is lucid dreaming. With Lucid Dreaming, you are conscious while dreaming. You know it is a dream.

The fourth type of multi-dimensional experience is called an out-of-body-experience, or OOBE. In an out-of-body experience, you are aware that you are out of your body and can navigate this or another world, not just a dream landscape. So, in this experience, you are not in a dream landscape, you are in the world. However, your abilities are limited- you can perceive the world, but you don't have a physical body to take significant actions. Through will, there have been minor physical actions, such as moving objects a little bit. This is the same as paranormal videos.

The fifth stage of multi-dimensional experience is what I call visiting heaven. The difference between visiting heaven and residing there is that the residents have adjusted and are comfortable, and I am just trying to get my bearings. This is the first stage where my experiences seem to differ from others.

Many who have had a near-death experience also visit heaven, during the NDE but also afterwards. People who have not had a NDE can and do visit heaven. But they may not remember it, or they may not understand what they experienced. The NDE becomes the opening of a door to the multi-dimensional experience.

In visiting heaven, I visit people I know whose bodies have died. Many are very surprised, because I don't think they have seen a living person conscious in heaven. They usually ask me how I do it and say something like I'm not supposed to be able to do that. I'm really not that good at it, I mean, I can see how I could be better at it. I get confused, I lose my way, I get distracted, I make small talk instead of getting what I'm there for, stuff like that.

The next stage of this type of experience is working with what you would call aliens. They come when

I summon them, but I don't really like these guys. They aren't typically built like humans, so they don't understand the nature of our bodies.

So, for example, some don't have pain, so you can operate on them while they watch, for instance. It's not a big deal till they want to see how you are built. "We'll put you back together the way you are after we're done" is not much comfort. I call this a different type of experience, and a unique one, because for me it is. When you make contact with these guys, they are the only ones in the room. You better know what you want, and if at all possible, be quick about it.

The next stage of this type of experience is working with my energetic body. My great teacher Yogananda was also able to do this type of work. I don't know that I'm closer to anyone than Yogananda, maybe my mom. At this level, you work with your energetic body and can observe it. This is how Yogananda was able to end his life on demand to show the west this truth.

It is common to call the connection of the soul to the body a silver cord. But it's not silver, it's energy. If you sever this cord you will die, but you must know how to do this as Yogananda did. That is more skill than I have. And the silver cord is only a small part of your energetic body, the connection between you and the energetic body which is controlling the body.

The next stage of this type of experience is to interact with entities. In Christian texts, these beings were called archangels. I have visited where they reside, but it was only because we wanted to see if I could handle it. I could not. I was not ready. If I could have handled it, I think I would be a much better off-world liaison, but I might not have come back here, too. There are a few waiting for me in heaven to give it another go, but I want to help humans first. At least, I must publish the transmissions. If anyone wants to get any of the stuff I can access, great.

The next experience is acquisition, for example, to work with others for the purpose of acquisition of tech. This is our goal. For this, we need a big village, and my challenge is to enable you to activate yourself properly. How big is what we are studying. Technically, a hundred thousand humans would do if they were properly activated. But I question if everyone in a group will be properly activated. At what level of diminished activation does the activation no longer work? At what level does the size of the group enable activation of everyone. So, for safety, we are thinking that 1 million for a project might work, and we're pretty sure that 3 million will work. That is our project.

The final experience is bilocation. This is like OOBE, except you manifest an image of yourself where you are located, which is not where your body is located, and can interact with those who are there. The most advanced ability is to interact with people who are there. You have the similar physical abilities as OOBE, meaning you cannot do much. I have not mastered this state. My training and skill set is focused on off-world abilities, so I haven't focused on OOBE and bilocation as much as acquisition.

These are the analyses the scientists I work with are studying off-world. It's a big project, a species can only go extinct once, and so the best shot is like, right now, when humans are closing in on the point of no return and enough humans can feel it, they know it.

There are the resources to do this. We added up everything and all the projects cost less than $200 billion, and the yield will be at least $2 trillion a year, so 10:1 annual return, or 1000%. So, we can do this. And this is just the return for investors. We estimate 10x increase in income for the most people. So, if you earn less than average household income, multiply your income by 10 to get our estimate of your potential income.

To do this, we use universal connections and symbols. This is my part of the project. These are the tools of the trade.

Normally, the off-world source with whom we work has considerable experience. The information is exchanged in symbols.

For a breathing human, the concept of symbols is the best I can do to describe the mechanism of communication off-world. This is important because symbols are how we can acquire technology and solutions. Symbols are the containers. The symbols, as well, have associated threads. These threads lead to other symbols.

Symbols of these types exist in the context of the individuals who created the symbol and their basis for the symbol. The symbol is passed in the contact with the individual who has created the symbol.

For solutions, which are different from technology, the off-world sources can work with threads, which are multi-connections, like a neuron which connects to multiple neurons.

As you can imagine, threadwork is quite complex, and quickly expands beyond workability, so we zoom in and out, in and out, and try not to lose the thread in the confusion of a dozen of options.

Think of Antman in the quantum realm, and I'm supposed to navigate this kaleidoscope, make a connection off-world, and have them hand me over some tech. That's where you come in, with you guys on the project and being clear about what you want, they don't even ask, it's amazing, they already know what I'm there for, they just hand it over, and I'm out of there. With any luck, I can make it work once I'm back. That is the plan.

Tech seems easy compared to solutions. But I don't have to bring back something technical, so that is simpler. With a solution, I must go off-world, find the ones who can help the solution take place. Then I have to come back to earth, find them, convince them, and we get a solution. But it is not just one person, it's a bunch of people who don't work with each other and are all over the place. Think of that Tom Cruise movie, Edge of Tomorrow, no matter how hard he tried, he couldn't convince the general to do something the general didn't want to do. That is how it is. But, again, your energy changes that like magic, if I a million help we've got a solution.

Summary

These types of experiences exist where a human is conscious and active without a body:

1.   Death

2.   Near Death Experience

3.   Lucid Dreaming

4.   Out of Body Experience

5.   Visiting Heaven

6.   Aliens Encounters

7.   Energetic Body

8.   Entities

9.   Acquisition

10.   Bilocation

The last six of this list will be used in this project, depending on the requirements of the project. There are two parts: acquisition off-world using one of these methods, and activation of humans.

Transmission

A transmission is the translation of a symbol into language. For example, when you feel love for someone, you translate this feeling into language, and may say or think, "I love you."

A symbol is an off-world concept. A symbol contains all supporting documentation. The translation of a symbol can go into as much detail or as little detail as desired. Some are small, with only a little translation required. Others are enormous.

I have had to decide how much of each symbol to translate so that a complete understanding can be achieved. If a translation is not adequate, please let me know and I can take another look at the symbol. I can add more to the transmission for the next version.

While this makes it seem like the symbol is a physical object, it is not. Additionally, the symbol typically has links to other souls and other symbols. To me, this is like depictions of neurons in the human brain with their several connections to other neurons.

Symbols

So, off-world we do not have memos. Memos are something you can say you did not get. Off-world, information is there, all you do is think about a subject and you get all the information, more info than you can handle in the next decade if you study full time.

I call this information a symbol. I had to pick a name or a description, so symbol works. Symbol in this context means all the information about a subject.

A symbol might include background info, history, probable pasts, comparative situations, every plan, all opinions, all analyses, all options, probabilities, probable realities, likely participants, participants behavior, participants contribution, with an alternative participants list that could be a thousand names on it with probable realities for each of their behaviors and contributions. Then there are connections to entire cultures of people who are oblivious to the situation and program because they choose to be. However, an asteroid hitting the planet will affect the dinosaur even if he does not care and pays no attention.